'Happy Birthday' Fan

by Karen Thomas

Remember the paper fans you made as a child? This is the same process, done more elegantly with a dollar bill.

MATERIALS: 1 new bill • 5" x 7" Green card • Cardstock (3⅛" x 6" Dark Blue Metallic, 2⅞" x 5½" Off White, 2" x 4⅝" Metallic Purple) • 4" Green mizuhiki cord • 4 Purple eyelets • Green marker • Eyelet tools • Scissors • Removable tape • Adhesive

INSTRUCTIONS:
1. Fold the fan. Wrap bottom of fan with cord.
2. Layer cardstocks and adhere to card.
3. Set eyelets.
4. Write "Happy Birthday" on bottom of card.
5. Adhere fan to card with removable tape.

MONEY TIPS

💲 Use extra large 'money' to practice folds.

💲 You can also use foreign money for a different look.

💲 By law, paper currency can only be photocopied in black & white, single-sided and must be reduced to 75% or enlarged to 150% of its original size.

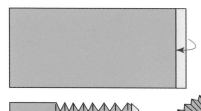

1. Fold the width of the White border on one end of the bill.

2. Accordion fold back and forth, keeping each fold the same width.

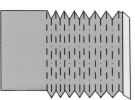

3. Pinch one end.

4. Loop the cord end and center over the end of the dollar.

5. Starting at the bottom, tightly wrap the cord around towards the loop. Thread the end through the loop at the top.

6. Pull end A from the bottom until tight. Trim excess cord B with scissors. Pull end A until loop and end B disappears under the wrap. Trim excess cord.

Small Frame
by Gay Merrill Gross

Frame your favorite photo in a patriotic presentation of support. This is a great memento for anyone serving our country.

MATERIALS:
2 new bills • 2 photos • Stickers • Cardstock (4¼" x 5½" Celery, 3¾" x 5" Dark Green, 2" x 4" Green) • 3" craft stick • Removable double-stick tape • Adhesive

INSTRUCTIONS:
1. Fold 2 frames, 1 with a photo.
2. Adhere Forest Green mat to Celery cardstock.
3. Cut out a Green clipboard top pattern. Adhere to top of mat.
4. Adhere flag sticker to craft stick. Adhere to mat.
5. Mat second photo and adhere as in photo.
6. Adhere stickers.
7. Adhere money frames with removable tape.

1. With face side up, make a mountain fold to the back. Your guide is the right edge of the vertical bar in the letter "E" in "UNITED". Crease sharply. Unfold.

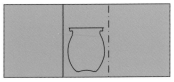

2. Repeat Step 1. Make a mountain fold at the end of the letter "F" in "OF". Crease very sharply. Unfold.

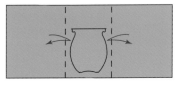

3. Change the 2 mountain creases to valley folds. Unfold.

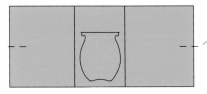

4. Pinch at the ½ mark on both short sides. Turn over.

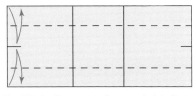

5. With Green side up, fold the long sides to the center. Crease sharply. Unfold. Turn over.

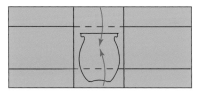

6. With face side up, fold on the Step 5 creases, folding sharply only at the center.

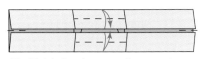

7. Fold the inner edges outwards, to the folded edges, creasing only in the center area.

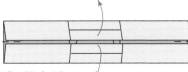

8. Unfold.

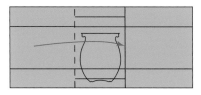

9. Put back the left vertical fold.

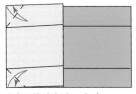

10. Fold the left corners to the horizontal creases. Unfold.

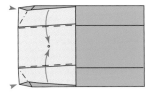

11. On the front layer, refold on the existing creases, at the same time accommodating at the left folded edge by squash folding the two triangles.

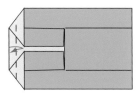

12. Flip the long flap to the left, bringing the edges of the triangles to the left folded edge. Unfold.

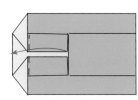

13. Fold the flap to the left, folding along the line where the flap meets the triangles.

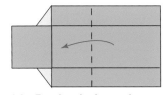

14. Put back the right vertical fold. Repeat Steps 10-13 on the right side.

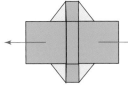

15. Holding each flap, pull them away from each other, forming a box in the center.

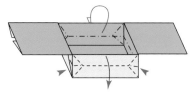

16. Insert photo if desired. Collapse the box by refolding on the existing creases and adding some new slanted folds.

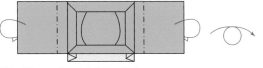

17. Note the width of the frame. Make a mountain fold parallel to each vertical crease, creating 2 sections equal in width to the frame width.

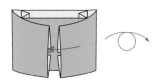

18. Bring the ends together and slide one inside the other forming a thin rectangular box.

PATTERN FOR
CLIPBOARD TOP

19. With 1 finger, press on George Washington's face so it touches the back of the frame.

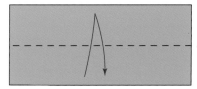

1. With face side up, fold bill in half. Unfold.

2. Turn the bill over. With Green side up, fold in half and unfold.

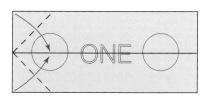

3. Fold the left corners to the center.

4. Fold the new folded edges to the center.

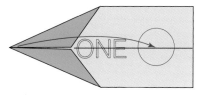

5. Fold the sharp left point to the middle of the circular seal.

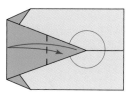

6. Fold the point back to the center of the left edge. Unfold.

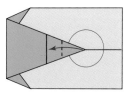

7. Fold the point back to the crease from Step 6.

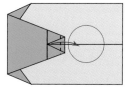

8. Fold the point to the right again, forming a narrow pleat.

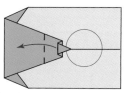

9. Fold again on the crease from Step 6.

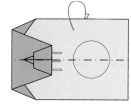

10. Mountain fold to the rear.

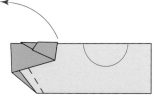

11. Lightly hold the head and slide the neck upward to the Step 12 position. Press flat the puffy fold at the bottom of the neck to hold this new position.

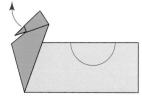

12. Lightly hold the head and slide it up to the position shown in Step 13. Press the new folds flat at the back of the head.

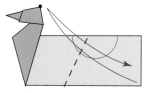

13. Fold the double corner at the bottom right to the top of the head. Crease sharply. Unfold.

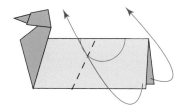

14. Spread open the bottom of the bird. Outside reverse fold the tail end upward by turning the end of the paper inside out and reflattening to Step 15 position.

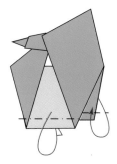

15. Mountain fold the bottom edge to the inside. Repeat behind.

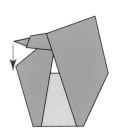

16. Holding the head, pull the beak downward and press it flat.

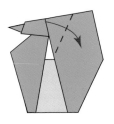

17. Blunt the loose tail corner. Repeat behind.

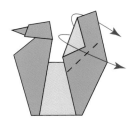

18. Outside reverse fold the end of the tail, turning it inside out, then flattening it.

19. Add bird to a card. For a tip, stand on a table or sit on the rim of a glass.

Bird on 'Best Wishes' Card

Card by Karen Thomas,
Bird by Gay Merrill Gross

Give your best wishes wings with a beautiful folded bird.

MATERIALS: 1 new bill • 4¼" x 5½" Olive card • 5½" square Celery cardstock • Forest Green marker • Craft knife • Removable double-stick tape • Adhesive
INSTRUCTIONS:
1. Fold the bird.
2. Cut a 2⅜" x 2⅝" window in the front cover of the card.
3. Cut Celery cardstock 4¼" x 5½" and adhere inside card.
4. Cut a piece of Celery cardstock 1" x 2½".
5. Write "Best Wishes" with Green marker and adhere to card.
6. Adhere bird inside the window with removable tape.

Variation for Bird's Tail

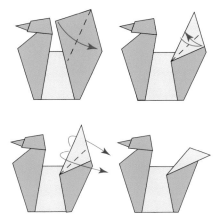

Blue Envelope

diagrams on page 13

Tree
Holiday Card

by Karen Thomas

Money does grow on trees - at least at Christmas time. This truly ever green tree is a gift in itself.

MATERIALS: 1 new bill • 5" x 6¾" Green card • Cardstock (4¼" x 4½" Gold, 1½" x 6¾" Red) • ⅜" Silver star • 36" mizuhiki cord • Rubber stamps (*Inkadinkado* Merry Christmas; *JudiKins* Background) • Gold embossing powder • Embossing ink • Heat gun • Bamboo skewer • Iron • Removable double-stick tape • Adhesive

INSTRUCTIONS:
1. Fold the money tree.
2. Press the tree with an iron on medium setting to flatten.
3. Emboss the background stamp on Gold cardstock.
4. Emboss "Merry Christmas" on Red cardstock.
5. Adhere Gold and Red cardstock to card.
6. Coil the mizuhiki cord around the skewer.
7. Wrap cord across the tree and adhere to back with removable tape.
8. Adhere tree to card with removable tape.
9. Adhere star in place.

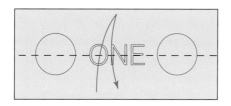

1. Fold in half lengthwise and unfold.

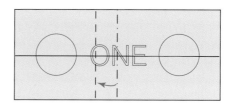

2. Mountain fold in the center and valley fold a little over the "O".

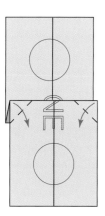

3. Turn 90°. Fold right and left corners at a 45° angle.

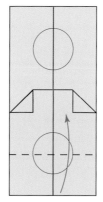

4. Fold bottom end up to meet bottom of folded corners.

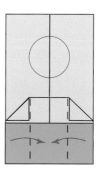

5. Fold right side to the center and squash fold the corner into a triangle. Repeat on left.

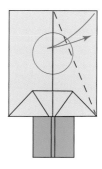

6. Fold top of tree down at an angle. Repeat on other side. Unfold.

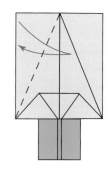

7. Repeat on other side. Unfold.

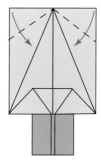

8. Fold down corners using the most recent folds as guides.

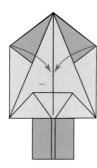

9. Refold sections to center line.

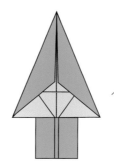

10. Turn completed tree over.

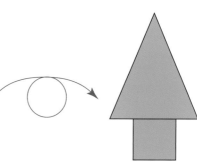

11. Add star to top and place on card.

Floating Dragon
'Thanks' Card

Card by Karen Thomas, Dragon by Gay Merrill Gross

The Asian dragon is traditionally celebrated for its benevolence, intelligence, and good will - a perfect symbol for expressing your gratitude on an attractive thank you card.

MATERIALS: 1 new bill • 5" x 6" Green card • 3" x 5" cardstock (Light Green, Forest Green) • Green Magic Mesh • Green fibers • Markers (Light Green, Dark Green) • Hole punch • Removable double-stick tape • Adhesive

INSTRUCTIONS:
1. Fold the dragon.
2. Cut Dark Green tag 2⅛" x 4¼". Cut a Light Green tag 2⅜" x 4½".
3. Punch a hole in the Dark Green tag. Thread fibers. Adhere to Light Green tag.
4. Adhere Magic Mesh and tags to card.
5. Write "Thanks" with Dark marker. Trace with Light marker.
6. Adhere dragon to card with removable tape.

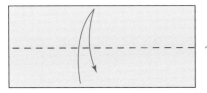

1. With Green side up, fold lengthwise in half and unfold. Turn over.

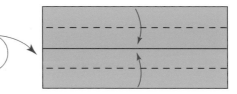

2. With face side up, fold the long sides to the center.

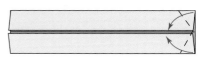

3. Fold the right corners to the center.

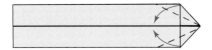

4. Fold the new folded edges to the center.

5. Fold the left edge to the top edge. Unfold.

6. Fold the left edge to the bottom edge. Unfold.

7. Fold the left edge behind, mountain folding through the crossing of the last 2 creases. Unfold.

8. Fold the left edge forward on the Step 7 crease.

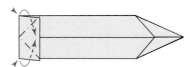

9. Press on the left corners, inside-reverse-folding them to the interior.

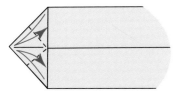

10. Fold the loose, narrow points to the left side corner. Unfold.

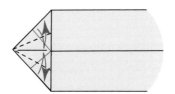

11. On the front layer only, fold the slanting edges to the center. Unfold.

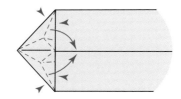

12. Pinch the loose flaps in half, forming 2 upright narrow points. Flatten points to the right.

13. Turn over, top to bottom, keeping the head on the left.

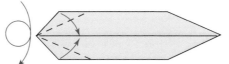

14. Fold short edges to the center.

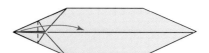

15. Fold the head inward along the fold line. The horns will flip out from the rear.

16. Mountain fold to the rear along the fold line shown.

17. Turn over top to bottom, keeping the tail end at the right.

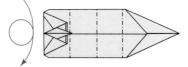

18. Make 3 mountain creases.

diagrams continued on page 12

diagrams continued from page 11

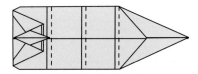

19. Make 3 valley creases, each slightly to the right of the mountain creases.

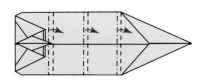

20. Use the 6 vertical creases to form 3 small pleats on the body.

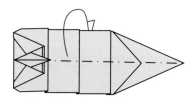

21. Mountain fold the top half behind the bottom half.

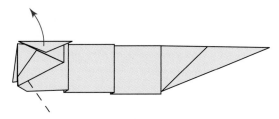

22. Lightly hold the head and slide the neck upward to the Step 23 position. Press flat the puffy fold at the bottom of the neck to hold this new position.

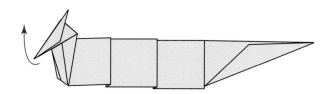

23. Lightly hold the head and slide it up to the position shown in Step 24. Press flat at the back of the head.

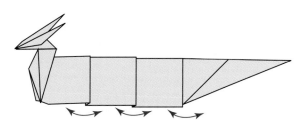

24. Stretch apart the lower end of each pleat. Press flat, giving a curve to the body.

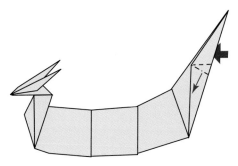

25. Open, flatten and lower the tail. Mountain fold it in half again in its new position, pinching it flat where it meets the body.

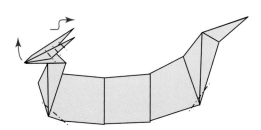

26. Press the nose against a table to give it a slight upturn. Lift each horn straight up and then pleat with a mountain and valley fold. Mountain fold the bottom corners inward. Repeat behind.

27. Optional: Bend bottoms toward inside on each side.

Optional: Wrap the body around a pen to give it a curve.

Wrapped Pencils

A pleasant surprise for teachers, graduates, and friends, these wrapped pencils fill the bill for any gift giving occasion.

MATERIALS:
1 new bill • Pencil • Removable double- stick tape
INSTRUCTIONS:
1. Curl bill around pencil.
2. Tape to secure.

Gift Envelope to Hold Bird

Karen Thomas

Tuck your folded bird into a unique envelope to add even more delight to your gift giving.

MATERIALS: 6" paper • Hero Arts rubber stamp "there are many good times ahead • Ink • Adhesive
INSTRUCTIONS:
1. Fold the envelope.
2. Print "there are many good times ahead on a scrap of paper and adhere it to the edge of the envelope.

Bird diagrams on pages 6-7

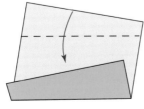

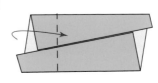

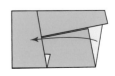

1. Fold up at an angle about ⅓ from the bottom.

2. Fold top down to the cut edge.

3. Fold the left side towards the center.

4. Fold the right side a little over the center.

5. Tuck tabs into pockets to lock envelope.

A Change of Heart

Card by Karen Thomas, Heart by Kathleen Weller

Oh Happy Day! Change a dollar bill into a heart that holds a quarter!

MATERIALS:

1 new bill • 4¼" x 5½" Ivory card • 4" x 5¼" cardstock (Olive, Celery) • Black marker • Craft knife • Removable double stick tape • Adhesive

INSTRUCTIONS:

1. Fold the heart. Insert quarter.
2. Adhere the Olive cardstock to the front of the card.
3. Cut an oval window in the front cover of the card.
4. Draw dashed lines around the edge of the Olive mat and window.
5. Write "Happy Day" on front of card.
6. Adhere Celery cardstock inside card.
7. Adhere heart inside the window with removable tape.

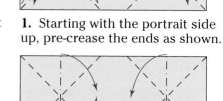

1. Starting with the portrait side up, pre-crease the ends as shown.

2. Fold a waterbomb base at each end of the bill.

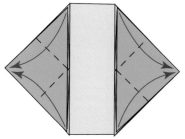

3. Valley fold top layer tips.

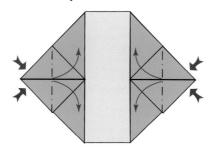

4. Squash fold each tip.

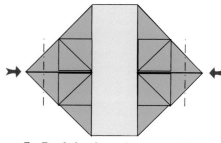

5. Push both ends inwards to create sink.

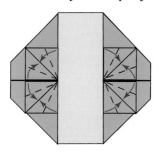

6. Valley fold the raw edges to the center lines of all 4 squares.

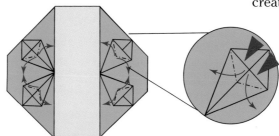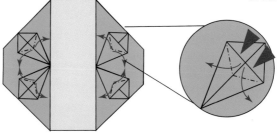

7. Squash fold the 8 small triangles. The area in the circle is detailed in Step 8.

8. Squash fold detail.

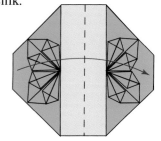

9. Valley fold in half.

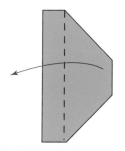

10. Valley fold the top layer.

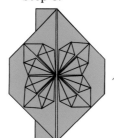

11. Turn the model over.

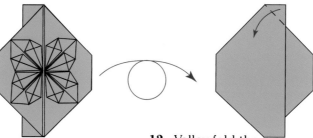

12. Valley fold the extended tip on top layer.

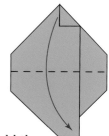

13. Fold the top part of the model down.

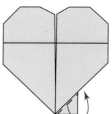

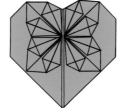

14. Valley fold the bottom corner over the inner flap to lock the heart. Turn over.

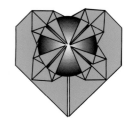

15. Carefully insert a quarter under the points.

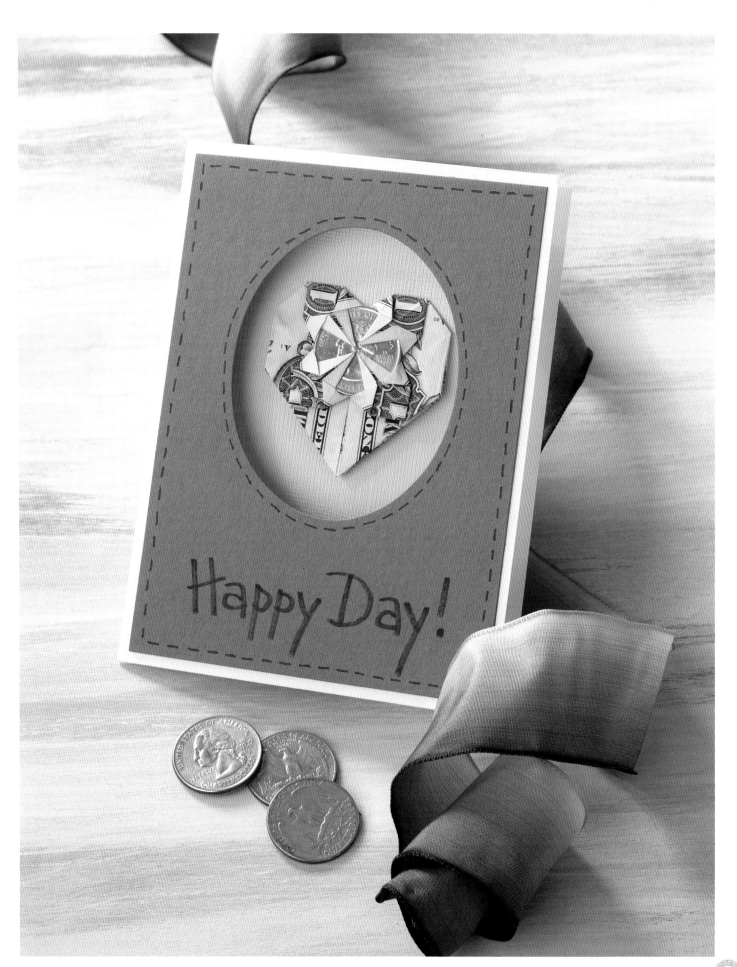

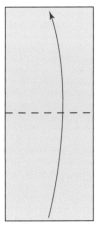

1. With face side down, valley fold short edge to short edge.

2. Valley fold the top, raw, short edge to and against one of the long edges. Unfold. The result is a 45° angle crease.

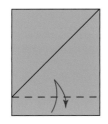

3. Valley fold the bottom folded edge up. The lower end of the 45° angle crease marks the level of the fold. Unfold the entire bill.

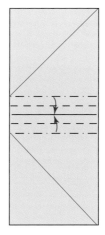

4. You will see three horizontal creases in the center area of the bill. Make the outer two into mountain creases (one already is). Valley fold these two mountain fold edges to the center crease line.

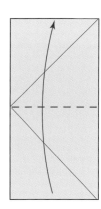

5. Valley fold the entire bill in half, short edge to short edge.

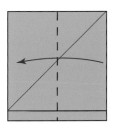

6. Valley fold in half, right double raw edge to left double raw edge.

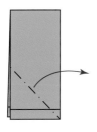

7. Squash fold by lifting the first two layers up and separating them evenly, to open a triangular pocket. Apply pressure to the layered center edge and press flat to the table.

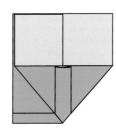

8. Turn model over and squash fold the other side.

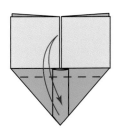

9. Valley fold bottom point up at the level of the printed border line of the bill. Unfold.

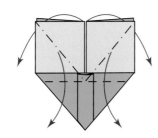

10. Squash fold the upper rectangular areas. Use the valley crease formed in Step 9 as a base line for this squash. Look ahead at the next step for clues to final shape.

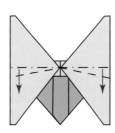

11. Work one wing at a time. Make a sharp mountain edge of the existing horizontal crease line, which runs across the center of the wing. Valley fold **some of the lower wing paper area** under this mountain edge. This will form a wing separation line, simulating a forewing and a hind wing. The lower or hind wing paper will change its shape when this is done. Look ahead to see the result. Repeat with the other wing.

Butterfly 'Thinking of You' Card

Card by Karen Thomas;
Butterfly by Michael LaFosse

A beaded butterfly comes winging your way bearing my happy thoughts of you!

MATERIALS: 1 new bill • 4½" x 7" Green card • 4" x 6½" Celery cardstock • 32 Green "e" beads • 8" mizuhiki cord • 6" Silver wire 20 gauge • Green marker • Removable double-stick tape • Adhesive

INSTRUCTIONS:
1. Fold the butterfly.
2. Fold mizuhiki cord in half. Wrap fold with tape to secure. Curl ends for antennae.
3. Curl one end of wire to stop beads from falling off.
4. Thread beads onto wire.
5. Tape end of wire to taped cord.
6. Secure taped portions behind the body of the butterfly.
7. Adhere Celery cardstock to front of card.
8. Write "Thinking of You" with Green marker.
9. Adhere butterfly with removable tape.

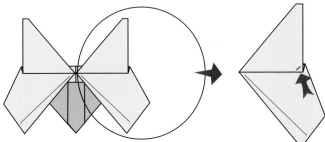

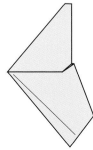

12. Give a rounded effect to the indicated corner by inside reverse folding it. The corner paper is pushed inside the paper layers and makes a V notch. Repeat with the other wing.

Shirt and Pants
'Be Who You Are' Card

Card by Karen Thomas, Shirt and Pants by Rachel Katz

Be who you are! This $2 pant suit is totally fashionable and really fun to make.

MATERIALS: 2 new bills • 5" x 7" Celery card • 3⅞" square "Be Who You Are" • 2⅜" x 4" Turquoise mat • Removable double-stick tape • Adhesive

INSTRUCTIONS:
1. Fold the shirt and pants.
2. Adhere Turquoise mat to the card.
3. Adhere "Be Who You Are" to the card.
4. Adhere shirt and pants with removable tape.

Shirt

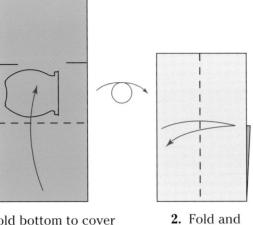

1. Fold bottom to cover face but not the thin line frame. Turn over.

2. Fold and unfold.

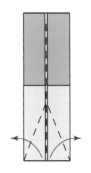

3. Fold sides to center.

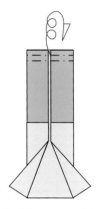

4. Fold outwards to form sleeves.

5. Mountain fold ¼" over and over.

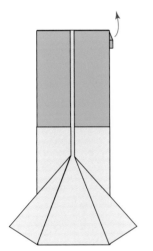

6. Unfold last mountain fold, leaving 1 mountain fold in.

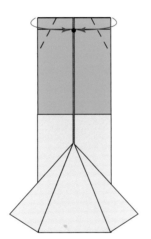

7. Collar: Top corners meet on the mountain fold line at the center dot.

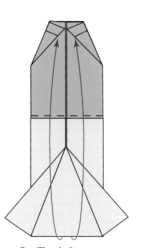

8. Tuck bottom under the collar. Press flat.

Shirt

Pants

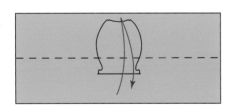

1. Fold in half lengthwise. Unfold.

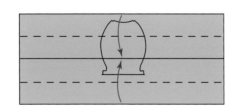

2. Valley fold long edges to center.

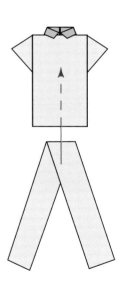

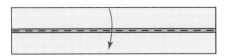

3. Valley fold lengthwise.

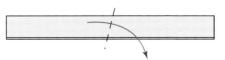

4. Valley fold at an angle.

Pants

Tip:
Tuck pants into the opening of the shirt.

'Love and Hope' Ribbon Card

by Karen Thomas

Send a message of love, hope and support with a folded memory ribbon card.

MATERIALS:

1 new bill • 5" x 6½" Pink card • Cardstock (4⅝" x 6⅜" Light Pink, 4" square Dark Pink, 5" square Forest Green) • Pink marker • Removable double-stick tape • Adhesive

INSTRUCTIONS:

1. Fold the ribbon.
2. Adhere ribbon to Forest Green cardstock with removable tape. Cut out cardstock ⅛" larger than ribbon.
3. Cut center squares of cardstock: 3" Forest Green and 2¾" Dark Pink. Stack squares and adhere to card.
4. Cut title mats: 1⅛" x 4" Forest Green and 1" x 3⅞" Dark Pink.
5. Adhere title mats to card.
6. Write "Love Hope" with a Pink marker.
7. Adhere ribbon with removable tape.

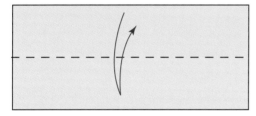

1. With face side down, valley fold bill in half. Unfold.

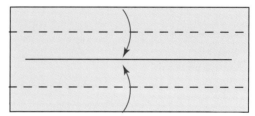

2. Cupboard fold the edges to the center.

3. Fold all 4 corners to the center crease.

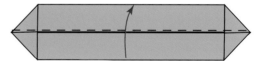

4. Valley fold up in half.

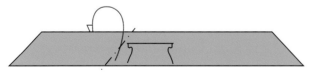

5. Mountain fold at an angle behind on the left side just a little outside of the portrait.

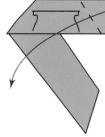

6. Valley fold at an angle on the right side just a little outside of the portrait.

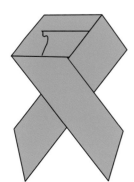

7. Bring right tail of ribbon under the left to lock them in position.

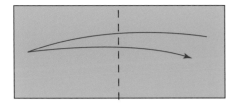

1. Fold bill in half. Unfold.

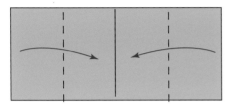

2. Cupboard fold two outside edges to center and crease.

Heart in a Heart Card

Card by Karen Thomas, Heart by Sy Chen

Enhance a romantic moment or create a heartfelt expression with a Heart in a Heart card.

MATERIALS:

1 new bill • 5" x 6¾" White card • Cardstock (3¾" x 5¼" Gold glossy, 8½" x 11" Red glossy) • Gold Chinese coin • Gold tassel • *JudiKins* Background rubber stamp • Black inkpad • Iron • Removable double-sided tape • Adhesive

INSTRUCTIONS:

1. Fold the heart.
2. Press the heart with an iron on medium setting to flatten.
3. Stamp the background on Gold cardstock.
4. Cut Red cardstock 5" x 6¾" and adhere to front of card.
5. Adhere Gold cardstock to card.
6. Cut a 3" square of Red cardstock and adhere to card.
7. Adhere tassel to card.
8. With removable tape, adhere heart to card over end of tassel.
9. Adhere coin in place.

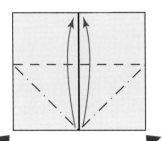

3. Precrease and then squash fold to form two large triangles that each lie along the center crease.

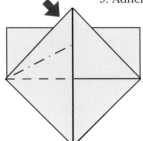

4. Lift flap up, open raw edges and squash flat to a kite shape.

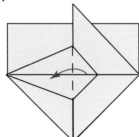

5. Fold top layer back along edge.

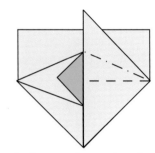

6. Repeat Steps 4 and 5 for right hand side.

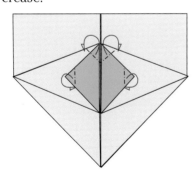

7. Fold points behind to create heart shape.

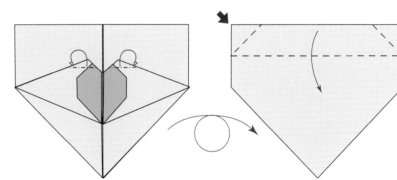

8. Fold top layers back and crease well. Turn over.

9. Fold top layer down, then open and flatten both corners.

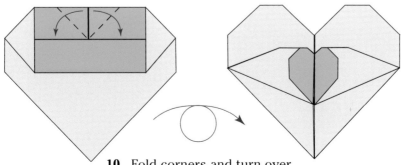

10. Fold corners and turn over.

Shirts

a traditional design introduced by
Toshie Takahama
This T-shirt has been in my col-
lection for almost 25 years. It is one
of the first things I ever folded.

MATERIALS:

1 new bill • 5" wire 20 gauge

INSTRUCTIONS:

1. For shirt with the portrait on the front, begin with the face down. For shirt with the "One" on the front, begin with the face up.
2. Fold the shirt.
3. Shape hanger following diagram.

HANGER DIAGRAM
Shape hangers from 20 gauge wire.

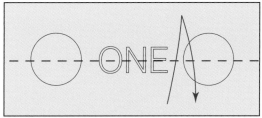

1. Valley fold bill in half and unfold..
TIP:
Make shirts different by starting with opposite sides of the dollar bill.

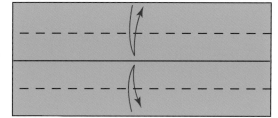

2. Cupboard fold long edges to the center. Unfold.

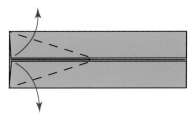

5. On the top layer only, valley fold angle creases at left edge to make sleeves.

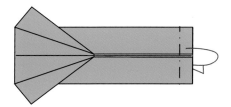

6. Mountain fold to the back about ¼".

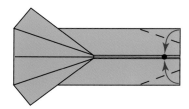

7. Valley fold to center to make the collar edge.

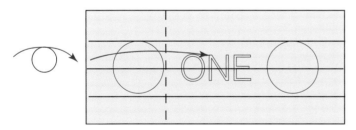

3. Valley fold the left edge at the outer edge of the seal circle.

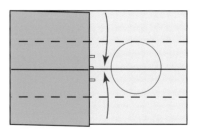

4. Cupboard fold to center on existing creases.

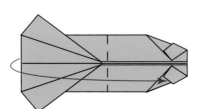

8. Fold left edge to tuck under collar points.

9. Done!

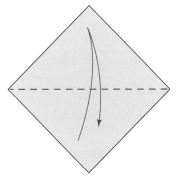

1. With printed side down, fold in half from corner to corner. Unfold.

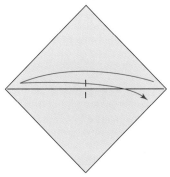

2. Make a pinch fold in the center by folding in half, but not creasing all the way.

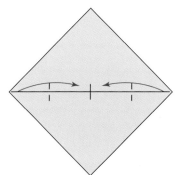

3. Make another set of pinch folds by bringing in outer points to center.

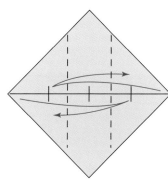

4. Bring left point to far right pinch-fold. Crease and unfold. Bring right point to far left pinch-fold. Crease and unfold.

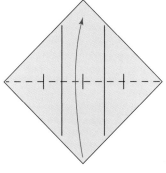

5. Fold paper along the first crease.

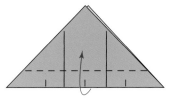

6. Fold the bottom ¾" up. This will determine the width and depth of bag.

7. Fold bottom right and left corners up to the side crease lines. Unfold and turn over.

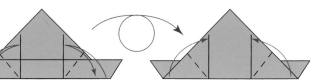

8. Fold bottom corners up again along same folds.

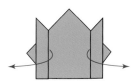

9. Unfold two right and left flaps.

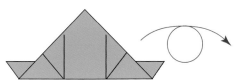

10. Turn the model over.

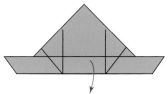

11. Fold bottom flap down and unfold paper completely.

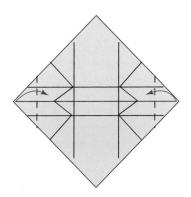

12. Fold corners in to the inner crease points.

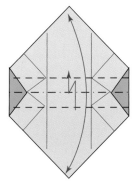

13. Pinch center crease up and fold layer up. Fold bottom layer up to top layer.

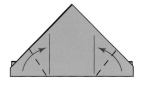

14. Fold up corners along existing creases.

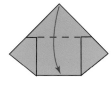

15. Fold top corners down.

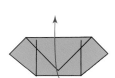

16. Unfold.

Money Bag

*bag design by
Makoto Yamaguchi*

*You can legally make
your own paper money by
photocopying a bill in
black and white, single
sided and enlarging it to
an 8" size.*

MATERIALS:
8" square play money • Adhesive

INSTRUCTIONS:
1. Cut play money into a 6" square
for bag and 2 strips ½" x 6" for
handles.

Ring diagrams on page 28

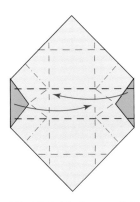

17. Unfold the model
except for the two
outer corners.

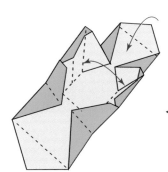

18. Collapse along
existing crease lines
to create bag shape.

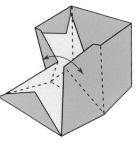

19. Fold top flap
down and secure with
a spot of glue.
Collapse along exist-
ing creases to create
other side of bag.

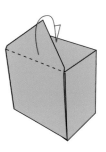

20. Fold top
flap down
along existing
crease and
glue in place.

21. Handles:
Fold in half
lengthwise. Glue
fold closed. Glue
handles to the
inside of the bag.

ONE DOLLAR 1

1. With face side down, mountain fold the top and bottom white borders only towards the face side. Mountain fold precisely in half lengthwise.

2. Mountain fold in half again.

3. The "One" will be evenly framed top and bottom with even White borders on the outermost edges.

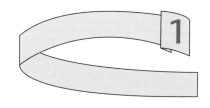

4. Mountain fold left edge border and mountain fold just outside the "1" for an evenly framed insignia. This will now be called the "head". The remainder will be called the "tail".

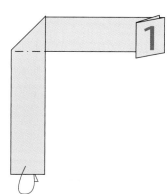

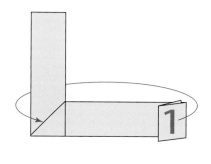

5. Start curving the bill away from the head as shown. Pay particular attention to the direction of the curve relative to the folds made in the head. If you curve the wrong way you won't be able to complete later steps. It helps to rub over the corner of a tabletop to get a nice curve out of a stiff bill.

6. Fold the tail at 90° about 2" away from the edge of the head. Curve around finger to make sure it fits. Mountain fold the vertical section of the tail to the rear and upward.

7. Make a 90° bend in the bill. Where this bend is made will determine the size of the ring. The further from the head, the larger the ring. Once you are accustomed to making these, you can wrap the curve around your own finger to estimate the correct position for this fold. Wrap the tail tightly. The portion to the left is shown in the same position as in the previous picture, and the tail folds underneath.

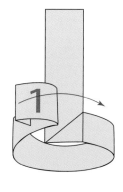

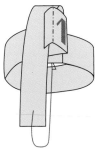

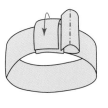

9. Tuck the white hem to the left of the head under the wrapped tail layers. Narrow the band of the ring by folding at the back towards center and tapering outwards.

8. Using the curve created in Step 6, loop the head back around to a position on top of the 90° bend made in the previous steps. Continue wrapping the tail around the body of the ring until all the excess length of the tail is used up. If you followed the previous steps closely, the very end of the tail will be on the outside of the ring under the bend in the head.

Dollar Ring

Project by Karen Thomas

from a traditional design

These instructions work well with $1 bills, $10 bills, and $50 bills. The ring can be made with fives and twenties, but require some adaptation due to the difference in the size and position of the denomination insignia.

MATERIALS: 1 new bill

Dollar Bill Gift Box

by Clay Randall

Who wouldn't love a present in a present? Give an unforgettable small gift, such as jewelry or a small origami, in a gift box made from money.

MATERIALS: 2 new bills

Dollar Bill Box

NOTE:

To make lid:
Fold exactly like the bottom except make the folds in Steps 1 and 2 in the box lid a little further out from the portrait frame, approximately 1/16" larger.

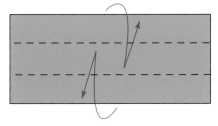

1. Make the Grid
Fold bill in thirds lengthwise and unfold.

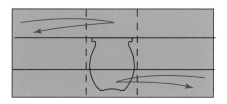

2. Valley fold the left side of the bill making the crease just outside of the portrait frame. Repeat on the right side of the bill.

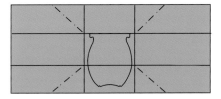

3. Put four diagonal mountain folds between the valley creases.

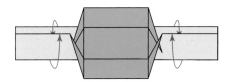

4. Using the existing creases, overlap the ends of the thirds and collapse into a box form.

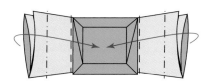

5. Fold flaps down and into box. Crease well.

Dollar Bill Fan

by Karen Thomas

Remember the paper fans you made as a child? This is the same process, done more elegantly with a dollar bill.

MATERIALS:
1 new bill • 4" Green mizuhiki cord

INSTRUCTIONS:
1. Fold the fan.
2. Wrap bottom of fan with cord.

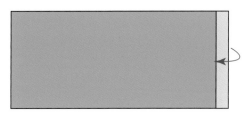

1. Fold the width of the White border on one end of the bill.

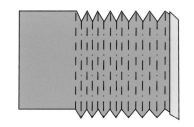

2. Accordion fold back and forth, keeping each fold the same width.

Green Gift Box diagrams on pages 32-33

3. Pinch one end.

4. Loop the cord end and center over the end of the dollar.

5. Starting at the bottom, tightly wrap the cord around towards the loop. Thread the end through the loop at the top.

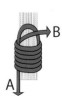

6. Pull end A from the bottom until tight. Trim excess cord B with scissors. Pull end A until loop and end B disappear under the wrap. Trim excess cord.

Bottom of Green Box

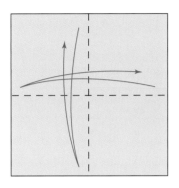

1. White side up, fold in half and unfold. Repeat in the other direction.

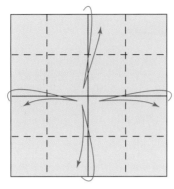

2. Fold each edge to the center and unfold.

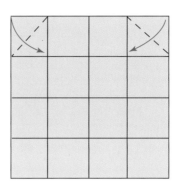

3. Fold each top corner to the nearest intersection point.

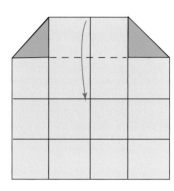

4. Refold down on the top horizontal crease.

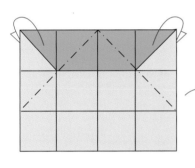

5. Turn over and fold each half of the top edge to the vertical center crease.

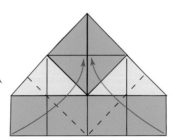

6. Fold each half of the bottom edge to the vertical center crease.

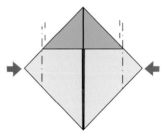

7. Inside reverse fold the side corners, inverting them between the front and rear layers.

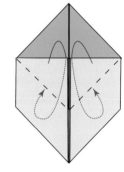

8. Lift the two loose corners and tuck each into the inner pocket beneath it.

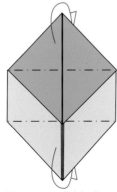

9. Mountain fold along the existing horizontal creases and unfold.

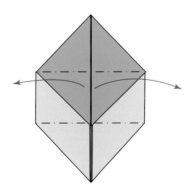

10. Separate the central edges and open the box.

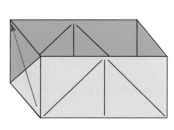

11. Straighten the sides of the box. Insert the tabs on the lid into the side pockets.

Green Gift Box

by Yukini Tanigawa and Minoko Ishibashi

Give a dollar bill box in a pretty green box as a surprise gift.

MATERIALS:
2 pieces of 6" x 6" origami paper

Top of Green Box

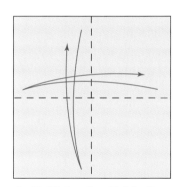

1 - 3 Make the Grid. Repeat steps 1 through 3 on page 32.

4. Refold down on the top horizontal crease. Unfold.

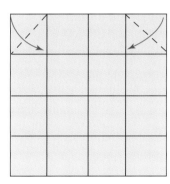

5. Fold the top edge down to the top horizontal crease.

6. Fold the right and left side edges to the center.

7. Make the precreases shown on the front layer. Open out to the boat shape shown in step 8.

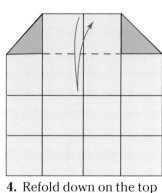

8. Fold the upper section down at the top edge of the boat. Unfold.

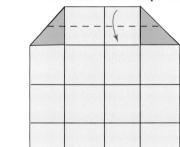

9. Separate the center edges and lay each along the top edge of the boat.

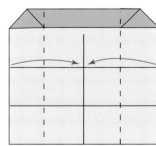

10. Fold the tabs up at a right angle.

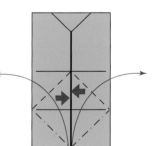

11. Insert the tabs into the side pockets on the box bottom.

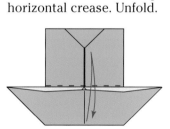

Tip: Dab adhesive inside to hold the tabs in place.

Folded Ornaments

adapted from a model by Didier Boursin

Deck the tree with ornaments that can be spent after the holiday. These variations are easily achieved just by leaving part of a fold open or changing the beads.

MATERIALS:
1 new bill • 10" White satin ribbon ½" wide • Assorted glass beads

INSTRUCTIONS:
1. Fold ornament.
2. Fold ribbon in half. Knot 1" below the loop.
3. String 2 beads on both ribbons. Knot.
4. String beads on tails. Knot to secure.
5. Close ornament around the ribbon.

1. Start with the face side down. Fold in half lengthwise. Unfold.

2. Valley fold bottom right corner to center crease. Fold at an angle so the crease ends at the top far right corner.

6. Fold all 3 points to opposite edges. Crease well. Unfold.

7. To make the ornament 3-dimensional, fold the left side along previous creases so that a small triangle flap is on top.